GEYSERS

What They Are and How They Work

SECOND EDITION

T. Scott Bryan

2005

Mountain Press Publishing Company

Missoula, Montana

Front cover photograph © 2005 by Pat Snyder
Beehive Geyser in Yellowstone National Park

Back cover photographs © 2005 by author
Top: Mortar Geyser in Yellowstone's Upper Geyser Basin typically
erupts once every several days but not at all during some years.
Middle: Spring Rustic-S6 in the Heart Lake Geyser Basin in Yellowstone National Park
Bottom: Lone Star Geyser in Lone Star Geyser Basin in Yellowstone National Park

Back cover background photograph: Steady Geyser in
Yellowstone's Lower Geyser Basin —NPS photo by George Marler

First edition published by Roberts Rinehart, Inc. Publishers in 1990
Second edition by Mountain Press Publishing Company in 2005

Library of Congress Cataloging-in-Publication Data
Bryan, T. Scott.
    Geysers : what they are and how they work / T. Scott
Bryan.—2nd ed.
        p. cm.
    Includes index.
    ISBN 0-87842-509-8 (pbk. : alk. paper)
    1. Geysers. I. Title.
    GB1198.5.B78 2005
    551.2'3—dc22   2005016748

PRINTED IN HONG KONG BY MANTEC PRODUCTION COMPANY

Mountain Press Publishing Company
P.O. Box 2399 • Missoula, MT 59806
406-728-1900

Contents

Baby Daisy Geyser, in Yellowstone's Upper Geyser Basin, is known to have only erupted for a few months in 1952 and 1959, then from February 2003 until December 2004, when it quit without warning.

Grand Geyser, the largest predictable geyser anywhere, sends bursts of water nearly 200 feet high as often as three times per day in Yellowstone's Upper Geyser Basin.

Major geyser basins of Yellowstone National Park.

Preface

Geysers is a book of wheres, whats, and hows. First describing where geysers are found, the book defines exactly what they are and develops the current understanding of how they work; how they relate to other geysers, other kinds of hot springs, and their environment; how they differ from one another; and how they change through the passage of time, including how human activities can and have already destroyed many geysers that used to exist. This information applies to all geysers wherever they are found in the world, but the focus is on Yellowstone National Park, Wyoming, where there are more geysers than in all the rest of the world combined.

This book presents the basic information a person needs to understand what geysers are all about, but only in general terms. It contains little about the actual activity—and personalities—of individual geysers. That knowledge is vital for anybody who wants to become a *geyser gazer*, a person who watches geysers and records the time and duration of eruptions, as well as other information about eruptions. For that, the most complete book is *The Geysers of Yellowstone,* also by T. Scott Bryan, which is frequently updated and includes descriptions of nearly every geyser in Yellowstone. The University Press of Colorado is planning to publish a thoroughly revised fourth edition soon.

Acknowledgments

Getting to know the geysers takes time. They are so dynamic and changeable that it might be impossible to ever become intimate with them, but at least an observer can learn geyser habits by geyser gazing—simple but careful observation combined with discussions about geysers with others who enjoy the pursuit. By making geyser gazing a community effort, all are able to maximize their learning. Many people are involved in the study of geysers, and it would be impossible to thank everybody who has participated. But a few special thanks are needed.

Employees of the National Park Service have produced most of the long–term data about geyser activity in Yellowstone National Park. Logbooks of geyser eruptions have been kept in the visitor centers for decades. Since about 1980, reports from geyser gazers have been added to these logs, data that is often more extensive than that produced by park employees, whose duties include many things other than geyser gazing. These logbooks are available for public viewing.

Most of the geyser gazers are individuals who visit geysers during their vacations. Banded together as the Geyser Observation and Study Association (GOSA), they produce a vast number of observations in a single summer. This data is passed along verbally, via the Internet, in a bimonthly newsletter, and in an annual volume of research papers. GOSA is an international organization, and the information it recently made available included current data about geysers in New Zealand, Chile, Kenya, and Iceland.

I would be remiss if I failed to thank the individuals who freely provided photographs for use in this book—Robin Renaut of Canada and Pat Snyder and Alan Glennon of the United States.

Last but foremost, of course, I give thanks to my wife, Betty, who not only has put up with my geyser gazing for more than thirty years, but who encouraged me to write this book in the first place.

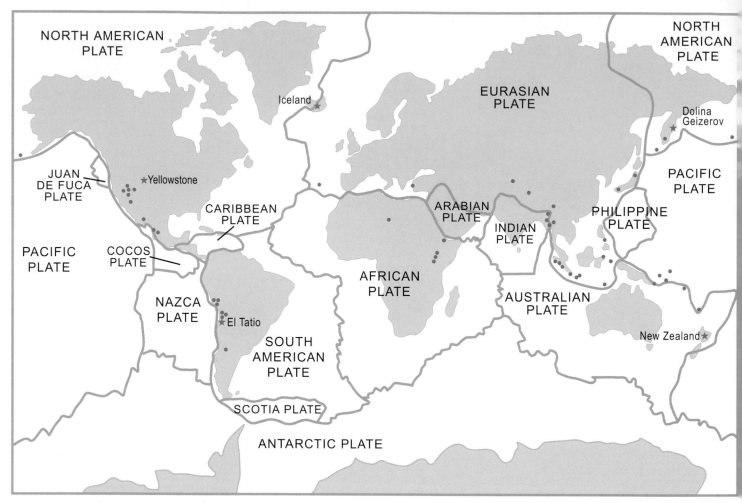

The five largest geyser fields (stars) and all other known fields (dots) *of the world are primarily located near the edges of tectonic plates.* See Geyser Fields of the World *in the back of this book for the name and location of each geyser field and information about each one.*

Where Geysers Are Found

Hot springs can be found in many regions of the world. Most have temperatures well below the boiling point of water. They can occur anywhere that water is able to penetrate deeply within Earth's crust.

Geysers and related high-temperature hot springs are much rarer. They require large volumes of boiling water and rock rich in silicon dioxide. Only in some geologically young volcanic areas are all of the necessary conditions met for geysers to function.

On the world map, you can see that geyser fields are concentrated along volcanic belts, linear regions where tectonic plates are converging upon one another or are splitting apart. Converging plate boundaries include the west coast of South America and parts of the west coast of North America, the western edge of the Pacific Ocean, and the eastern side of the Indian Ocean. Regions where a plate is splitting include the

New Zealand's Waimangu Geyser, whose name means "Black Water," was by far the largest geyser ever known. Active only between 1900 and 1904, some eruptions reached over 1,500 feet high. —Photographer unknown

Known only as Geyser T-1 at Beowawe, Nevada, this was one among more than thirty geysers at what was one of the world's premier geyser fields before the construction of a geothermal power plant in the 1980s destroyed it.

Geyser 42w at Steamboat Hot Springs, just south of Reno, Nevada, erupted over 20 feet high before it and all the other geysers there were destroyed by a power plant that began producing electricity from geothermal steam in 1986.

mid-Atlantic ridge and the East Africa rift valley. The Yellowstone geyser field is an exception—it sits above a hot spot, a place where a plume of magma is welling up from deep within Earth. The geyser fields in Nevada and Oregon are areas where the crust has been stretched, and fault zones allow water to circulate deeply.

Hundreds of volcanoes have been active during human history, and there are many additional youthful volcanic areas, but geysers are known to exist in only about forty of these places with another twenty or so locations with now-extinct or undocumented geysers. These special spots are called *geyser fields*.

Pohutu Geyser, joined by the Prince of Wales Feathers jetting to its left, is the largest and most consistently active geyser in New Zealand. It is at Whakarewarewa just outside the city of Rotorua.

In 1991, Grot Yubileinyi was the most powerful geyser in Dolina Geizerov, the "Valley of Geysers" on Russia's Kamchatka Peninsula. Some of its eruptions reached as far as 200 feet outward from a cavernous vent in the mountainside.

Spring KL6, on the shoreline of Lake Bogoria in Kenya, played as a geyser during the 1990s, erupting up to 10 feet high.
—Robin Renaut photo

Earthquake tremors occasionally trigger geyser eruptions at Ho[t] Creek in California's Lo[ng] Valley Caldera, such as those witnessed at "Hot Creek Geyser." The eruptive activity tends to die down quickly, a[nd] often no geysers can b[e] seen there.

Yellowstone National Park is by far the biggest geyser field of all, with more than five hundred geysers, including those with such famous names as Old Faithful, Giant, Riverside, Grand, and Castle Geysers. Yellowstone contains at least half of all the geysers on Earth! In *all* the rest of the world not more than five hundred geysers remain.

The best-known geyser fields elsewhere are in Iceland, the site of Geysir (the namesake of all geysers) and Strokkur; and in New Zealand, home of Pohutu Geyser and Waimangu (once the largest geyser ever known). These areas used to include many geysers and could be compared to Yellowstone, but most of their geysers ceased to erupt because of both natural events and human activity. Less well known, but with more active geysers, are the fields in the Kronotsky Nature Reserve on Russia's Kamchatka Peninsula, and at El Tatio in Chile. In these four places combined there might be as many as four hundred active geysers.

There used to be two world-class geyser fields in Nevada. Beowawe in the north-central part of the state was once proposed as a national park. More than thirty of its fifty hot springs were geysers, the greatest concentration of geysers anywhere. Some erupted over 30 feet high. Steamboat Hot Springs, just south of Reno, included two dozen geysers. Most were small but three that erupted as high as 50 to 75 feet attracted considerable attention during the early 1860s. Unfortunately, geothermal power plant developments in each of these areas destroyed their geysers during the 1980s.

That leaves only about one hundred geysers among all the other geyser fields on Earth. The typical geyser field therefore contains only a few geysers.

Geysers are very important members of the volcanic systems they are a part of. Their rarity tells scientists a great deal about the geology and conditions below the surface, so they have been studied wherever they have been found. But just as important is their fascinating and beautiful activity. They are one of the best examples of "living geology," and they are easy to understand.

El Tatio, a geyser field at nearly 14,000 feet high in the Andes Mountains of Chile, means "the grandfather" in the native Indian language. Its largest geyser, known simply as Geyser T-25, jets water up to 25 feet high near the equipment of an abandoned water desalinization experiment. —Alan Glennon photo

Hot Springs of the Geyser Fields

Geyser fields contain different kinds of hot springs—fumaroles, mud pots, pools, and geysers. Which kind will show up at a specific spot depends not only on how much water is available to the spring but also on how hot the water is, the size and shape of the subsurface plumbing system, and its subsurface connections with other individual hot springs.

Fumaroles, also called *steam vents*, exist when there is so little subsurface water at such a high temperature that it completely boils away below ground. All that is left is the steam. There may be some small amounts of other gases along with the steam, such as hydrogen sulfide, which causes the rotten egg odor of the geyser basins, and carbon dioxide. Fumaroles are best viewed in cool weather

An unnamed vent among the Porcelain Springs at Norris Geyser Basin is a typical fumarole, emitting only steam and other volcanic gases.

when the superheated vapor quickly condenses into billowing clouds of steam.

Fumaroles are usually static. They don't change their appearance very much, and they always do essentially the same thing. Fumaroles are the hottest of all hot springs, and most are superheated (hotter than boiling). The temperature of steam in Yellowstone has been measured as high as 238 degrees Fahrenheit, considerably higher than 198 degrees Fahrenheit, the temperature at which water boils at Yellowstone's elevation.

Mud pots are fumaroles that have been drowned beneath surface water, which keeps the steam and other gases from escaping directly into the atmosphere. The hydrogen sulfide is oxidized in the water by chemical reactions and by primitive bacteria and archaea, such as *Sulfolobus*, to form sulfuric acid. The solution becomes as strong as battery acid and attacks the rock lining of the hot spring crater. The disintegrating rock creates the wet clay of the mud pot.

The fumarole beneath the mud is always there, and it makes the bubbles of steam that cause the boiling and bursting action of the mud pot. The amount of surface water constantly increases and decreases since it comes from rainfall and snowmelt, so the consistency of mud pots changes throughout the year. The thin slurry of a paint pot in spring might become the pasty, cementlike mud of a mud volcano by autumn, and occasionally a mud pot dries out completely and reverts to a fumarole.

Mud pots undergo dramatic changes through the year, often being thin paint pots in spring and early summer but then drying out to become mud volcanoes during the hot, dry summer and fall. These mud volcanoes are in Yellowstone's Microcosm Basin in the Lower Geyser Basin.

The mud pot known as Muddy Sneaker was a short-lived feature at Yellowstone's Norris Geyser Basin.

As the dry summer season progressed, the water level dropped and terraces developed within the crater of this unnamed mud pot in Yellowstone's backcountry.

Near Niland, California, there are several areas with small mud pots and mud volcanoes near a geyser field that now lies under the water of the Salton Sea.

Bone Pool in Yellowstone's Gibbon Geyser Basin is typical of the noneruptive hot spring called a pool, where its high temperature and overflow keep the quiet water clean and pure.

Pink Cone Geyser in Yellowstone's Lower Geyser Basin has water jets that reach up to 30 feet high during eruptions that last as long as 1¹/₂ hours.

Pools are hot springs in which enough subsurface water comes to the surface to keep the fluid from entirely boiling away. The continual supply of water is enough to carry away any mud and debris that enters the crater. The temperature of the water is usually close to the boiling point, so it will not support colorful growths of algae or bacteria, or become stagnant, and it is alkaline and does not attack the crater walls.

The water in a pool is often of remarkable purity. However, some dissolved minerals and gases are present and can include arsenic and sulfur, so drinking the water is not a good idea. But the water is clear. Sometimes it's easy to count the pebbles on the bottom of a crater that is more than 40 feet deep.

The color of pools can also be beautiful. The rich azure and turquoise shades are not the result

The crater of Grand Prismatic Spring in Yellowstone's Midway Geyser Basin is 270 feet wide, making it the single largest hot spring pool in the world.

of minerals dissolved in the water or because of a reflection of the sky, but simply because the water is clean. As with lakes and oceans, the water in the pools looks colored because it absorbs all the colors of the light spectrum except the blues and greens. The exact tint depends on the depth and volume of the body of water plus any color in the walls of the spring's crater.

Geysers are the most special and unusual of all hot springs. Geysers erupt, jetting their water into the air, often to only a few inches but sometimes to remarkable heights. They erupt because of very special geological conditions involving a large volume of boiling water within a confining space. What geysers are and how they work is discussed later, but first let's see what lives in hot spring water.

As the water flows farther from its source and cools, the color of cyanobacteria grows darker, from yellow through orange to brown.

Watermelon Geyser, a small perpetual spouter at the bottom of the Grand Canyon of the Yellowstone, supports a profuse growth of cyanobacteria. A landslide in the 1970s destroyed much of the trail to it, which is now closed.

Can Anything Live in This Water?

The variety of life that survives in hot spring water—*thermophilic life*—is incredibly diverse. Just what lives in a given place depends on the temperature of the water and whether it is acidic or alkaline.

Hot spring water usually contains little dissolved mineral matter, and practically the only mineral deposited by the water is pale gray to white geyserite, a hydrated silicon dioxide. Therefore, most of the colors you see in the geyser basins are caused by forms of life. Most obvious are cyanobacteria (previously known as blue-green algae) such as *Synechococcus* and *Chloroflexus*. These primitive organisms, which evolved early in Earth's history, can survive in water as hot as 167 degrees Fahrenheit, at which temperature the cyanobacteria growth is pale yellow. As the water temperature drops, the color darkens and progresses through a range of oranges to dark brown. At about 120 degrees Fahrenheit the cyanobacteria is replaced by true algae with a rich green color. Exposed bacterial mats are home to colonies of ephydrid flies and spiders that survive year-round in the protective warmth.

Water that is even hotter—up to and even above the boiling temperature of 198 degrees Fahrenheit at Yellowstone's elevation above sea level—can support *true bacteria*. One of these bacteria, thriving at 170 degrees Fahrenheit, is *Thermus aquaticus*. Look for stringy, pale yellow or pale pink growths in the runoff channels of boiling pools. Discovered in Yellowstone's Lower Geyser Basin but now known worldwide, it is the source of Taq DNA Polymerase, an enzyme used to copy and amplify DNA for medical diagnosis, criminal forensics, and genetic fingerprinting.

Thermus aquaticus, *a stringy pink growth, is a bacterium that was discovered in Yellowstone's Lower Geyser Basin.*

Though it resembles Thermus aquaticus, *this is just one of numerous other bacteria that have been discovered living in the near-boiling runoff channels of many Yellowstone hot springs.*

The warm runoff water in acidic thermal areas, such as Yellowstone's Norris Geyser Basin, supports the growth of rich green Cyanidium, *one of the true algae.*

Some geyser basins, such as Yellowstone's Norris Geyser Basin as well as any mud pot area, have acidic water. There, mineral deposits, especially yellowish brown iron oxide, cause most of the bright colors. Thermophilic organisms are less common, but a bright green mat is usually *Cyanidium,* one of the true algae. Acidic springs can also support varieties of archaea. One of these, known only as "PjP78," thrives in an acidic pool in Yellowstone's Hayden Valley and is believed to be the living organism most closely related to the primordial origin of life. Especially common is *Sulfolobus,* another archaea that metabolizes elemental sulfur into sulfur oxides, which become sulfuric acid when mixed with water, producing the strongly acidic conditions of mud pot areas.

What Is a Geyser?

Exactly what is meant when one says "geyser" depends on the definition one uses. A rigorous and technical definition developed by geologists with the U.S. Geological Survey and now adopted in most nations around the world reads like this:

> A geyser is a hot spring characterized by intermittent discharge of water ejected as a turbulent eruption that is accomplished by a vapor phase.

Geysers are rare enough to attract attention wherever and whenever they are discovered. Here are some of Yellowstone's first tourists, closely (too closely!) examining the cone of Beehive Geyser. Behind them is the tent camp of the Yellowstone Park Improvement Company, established in 1883 as the first large-scale lodging facility at Old Faithful. —NPS photo, photographer unknown

What sounds simple is not necessarily so. Here's what the terms within the definition mean:

First, a geyser is a *hot spring*. Some erupting cold-water springs (so-called soda-pop geysers) have eruptions powered by carbon dioxide gas, but these are not true geysers. Any bona fide geyser erupts water at a temperature near and usually hotter than boiling.

Second, a geyser is an *intermittent*, or *periodic*, spring. It does not erupt all of the time. Geysers always spend some of the time quietly recovering from one eruption and preparing for the next.

Third, the eruption must be *turbulent*. That means forceful, not quiet. To be classified as turbulent, an eruption does not have to reach any minimum height. The most common way of determining turbulence is whether or not the water surface is broken by the activity. A few inches can be big enough, at least according to some observers.

Finally, the action is powered by pressure from the *vapor phase* of gases rising from below. In a hot spring, the gas is mostly steam, so boiling has to take place below the surface.

This definition sounds like it might exclude a lot of hot springs from the realm of geysers, but most candidates have no trouble meeting the requirements of the definition. Some, however, come close but don't quite make it.

Hot Springs That Look Like Geysers but Aren't

Three kinds of hot spring common to geyser basins look like geysers but fail to fit the definition.

Intermittent springs are periodic, like geysers, and they operate because of a vapor phase forming below the surface. But they are too weak to be geysers. Instead of erupting turbulently, they simply overflow quietly every now and then.

There is some uncertainty in the distinction between geysers and intermittent springs. Many geysers quietly overflow at times between their eruptions, but since they finally do erupt, they are true geysers. Who can say for certain that an intermittent spring doesn't also have rare, unseen eruptions? If so, even if just one time, it would be a geyser.

Perpetual spouters, on the other hand, definitely do erupt. The trouble with them is that their eruptions never stop, so they are not periodic. Perpetual spouters can be beautiful and as big as large geysers, and here again there is some controversy about their status. Several so-called perpetual spouters are known to have erupted continuously for years, only to stop for a few hours or days and then restart. Yellowstone's aptly named Steady Geyser, for example, erupted continuously for at least one hundred years before stopping a few times in 2004. Other spouters have occasional pauses of only a few seconds within otherwise constant activity. There is no definition as to how long an inactive period has to be, so it is possible that all perpetual spouters could be defined as geysers—and they often are.

The question of whether a perpetual spouter could be a geyser might not be important in a place like Yellowstone where there are hundreds of geysers. However, geologists do not include Zunil, Guatemala, on the list of geyser fields because its impressive spouters, as much as 30 feet high, have *never* been observed to pause; they are not geysers.

Is Cyclops Spring in Yellowstone's Upper Geyser Basin a simple intermittent spring, or is it a geyser? It apparently erupted a few times after the earthquake of 1959, but otherwise its amount of overflow only varies slightly.

Steady Geyser in Yellowstone's Lower Geyser Basin was the epitome of perpetual spouters, in that it was never known to stop erupting—until 2004, when it began to have occasional pauses that lasted for hours during its eruption. —NPS photo by George Marler

Other erupting features exist, too. Around the western United States there are several so-called geysers that actually are nothing more than water wells that erupt because they happened to strike boiling water. Some, such as Old Faithful Geyser of California in Calistoga are touted as having almost magical properties, while Old Perpetual Geyser near Lakeview, Oregon, erupts in front of a motel. In Yellowstone, wells drilled for research purposes have erupted during their construction, but all of them are now capped and inactive.

Soda-pop geysers erupt ice cold water and are powered by the release of carbon dioxide gas. Small natural springs of this sort exist in Pennsylvania, the Czech Republic, and Azerbaijan. Utah's Crystal, Woodside, and Champagne "geysers" and Idaho's Captive Geyser are drilled wells that erupt for the same reason. Even Yellowstone boasts a soda-pop geyser, Cold Water Geyser near Mud Volcano.

Here and there, too, are springs that jet water into the air because of artesian pressure in a subsurface aquifer. Sometimes these spout hot water. Examples of these include the "geysers" near Cisolok, Indonesia, the Chimanimani Geyser of Zimbabwe, and springs along the Masy River in Madagascar.

Although these features do erupt and sometimes spectacularly, they are not true geysers.

The billowing clouds
steam that rise fr
Porcelain Basi
Yellowstone's No
Geyser Basin
proof of abund
water supplies a
potent heat sourc

Excelsior Geyser in Midway
Geyser Basin has not had a
major eruption since 1890,
when some of its bursts
reached more than 300 feet
high and were nearly that
wide. Now it is Yellowstone's
single greatest source of
geothermal water,
discharging nearly 6
million gallons per day.
—NPS photo by
F. J. Haynes in 1888

Geological Requirements for Geyser Activity

Geysers are rare because a special set of geological conditions has to be met in order for them to exist. These conditions don't sound so unusual, and they aren't if taken individually. The combination of them is what makes geysers so unique.

Water Supply

Geysers require enormous amounts of water. Measurements show that the volume of water discharged within Yellowstone's Upper Geyser Basin, which includes Old Faithful, amounts to at least 12 million gallons per day. That's more than 8,000 gallons in every minute of every day. Some individual geysers put out tens of thousands of gallons of water with every eruption. And remarkably, these values are for liquid water only. The equivalent volume of water vapor (steam) lost by the hot springs is probably as great.

Almost all of this water started out on Earth's surface as rain or snow. In Yellowstone as anywhere else, most snowmelt and rain runs across the land surface, down the rivers, and to the oceans. Perhaps less than 5 percent manages to trickle below the surface and into the geothermal system. Yet that small amount is the water supply for all of Yellowstone's hot springs. Geochemical studies indicate that the total volume of water discharged by *all* of Yellowstone's hot springs combined is more than 600 million gallons per day. For an area to have geysers, it must have abundant precipitation. Yellowstone, on the Continental Divide, is a magnet for storms and receives considerable winter snow that seeps into the ground as it melts.

Although the hot springs of a geyser basin might occur within a small area, the geothermal field covers a wide region. In Yellowstone, some of the thermal water may originate in the Madison Range, more than 35 miles northwest of Old Faithful and outside of the national park.

Volcanic Heat Source

Because geysers require great volumes of hot water that starts out as cold surface water, there must be a very strong heat source beneath a geyser basin. For example, according to studies by the U.S. Geological Survey, the actual value for the amount of heat released by the entire Yellowstone system works out to more than 70 *trillion* calories per day. That's enough to melt more than *1 million tons* (2 *billion* pounds) of ice every day, or more than 23,000 pounds per second! The only possible source for this much heat is volcanic activity.

How the heat gets into the water is simple. The cold water from the surface slowly trickles through the rocks below ground. Eventually it reaches a depth of as much as 13,000 feet below the surface. Because geyser fields are in young volcanic areas, these rocks are still hot. The water is heated by its contact with the rocks and actually gets as hot as 650 degrees Fahrenheit. It stays liquid rather than vaporizing into steam because it is under great confining pressure from the rocks and water lying above.

The movement of the water in a geothermal system is very slow. Never, except within the hot springs themselves, are there open channels for the water to flow through. Instead, water just percolates through tiny cracks and around mineral grains in the rock. The entire trip from the surface and back probably takes at least 1,100 years. The water you see erupting in Yellowstone today fell as rain and snow long before Columbus explored the New World, maybe even in the days of Julius Caesar!

Geyserite

Geysers erupt because their plumbing systems are pressure tight. If they weren't, they could not sustain the force necessary to throw water into the air. The rocks just below the ground within geyser basins are mostly sand and gravel deposited by rivers. But if there were only sand and gravel below, hot springs would leak the pressure and geysers would not exist.

At greater depths below geyser fields, where the temperature is high and the pressure is great, water dissolves some of the minerals from the rock. It isn't very much. In the case of Old Faithful Geyser in Yellowstone, where detailed studies have been done, only about 1,000 pounds of minerals per day is brought to the surface in the water, about the same concentration as in your tap water at home. Most of this mineral is silicon dioxide, or *silica*.

Pure silica, which occurs in nature as the mineral quartz, is not very soluble in water. Even in a geothermal system only a small amount is actually dissolved. Yet enough of this mineral must be brought to the surface to seal in a geyser, so the rock that the superheated water passes through must be very rich in silica. The kind of volcanic rock that can provide enough silica is called *rhyolite*. It is the chemical equivalent of granite but formed after the magma reached the surface of Earth, unlike granite, which cools below the surface. Rhyolite typically has small crystals of quartz and feldspar in a finer-grained matrix, though sometimes it is glassy.

Rhyolite, a very ordinary volcanic rock, is the source of the silica that forms geyserite.

The glassy forms of rhyolite, such as obsidian and pitchstone, are chemically identical to the granular form, but the volcanic lava cooled so fast that crystals did not have time to form.

As long as the water stays at high temperature and pressure, the silica stays in solution, but when it flows through the more-open plumbing of a hot spring, some silica is precipitated along the way as *geyserite*, or *siliceous sinter*, a lightweight, porous deposit made of hydrated silica. The geyserite that forms below the surface seals the plumbing systems within the unconsolidated sand and gravel, but you can see the stuff everywhere at the surface in a geyser basin. It creates the geyser cones, platforms, and barren terraces among the hot springs.

Geyserite deposits often form intricate patterns of ridges and beads.

The terraces of geyserite at Old Faithful Geyser.

Iron oxide lines an unnamed pool at the Norris Geyser Basin.

Geothermal areas often contain mineral deposits in addition to geyserite, such as the iron oxide–rich cones of Yellowstone's Chocolate Pots.

Almost all of the silica contained in the water is simply carried away by the geyser's runoff. Only a little goes into forming the geyserite, so the deposits develop slowly. The rate of formation varies, but most deposits probably grow less than 1 inch per century. Please do not think of collecting them. If taken home, specimens will quickly dehydrate and collapse into dust, yet nature will require a great many years to replace what was lost.

Though geyserite is commonly considered critical to the existence of geysers, other minerals often form deposits within geothermal areas and can seal the plumbing enough to support small geysers. Travertine (calcareous sinter) hosts the geysers at Lake Bogoria, Kenya, and the spouting springs of Cisolok, Indonesia. Sinter rich in iron oxide (ferric sinter), perhaps similar to Yellowstone's Chocolate Pots, reportedly occurs at an unidentified geyser locality in Xizang, China. Indeed, a few geysers are known to erupt directly from volcanic bedrock where there apparently are no mineral deposits at all.

Plumbing System

Any hot spring must have a network of underground fractures and channels that provides it with water. This plumbing system is usually open enough to allow the water that enters at the bottom to flow freely to the top, but a geyser must have a narrow spot or constriction at some point, usually close to the surface. Water pooled above the constriction acts like a lid, helping maintain the pressure on the boiling water below. When the geyser finally does erupt, it acts like a pressure cooker without a relief valve—it blows off its lid and shoots skyward.

The size of a geyser determines how small the constriction has to be. In some of the larger ones it might be several feet across, but most constrictions are only a few inches wide.

In summary, only four simple things are necessary to have a geyser—the right water volume, heat supply, rock chemistry, and plumbing shape. It is the combination of these four things that is rare.

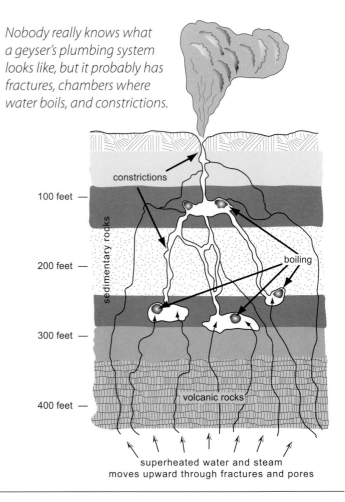

Nobody really knows what a geyser's plumbing system looks like, but it probably has fractures, chambers where water boils, and constrictions.

constrictions

100 feet —

sedimentary rocks

boiling

200 feet —

300 feet —

volcanic rocks

400 feet —

superheated water and steam
moves upward through fractures and pores

How Geysers Erupt

A geyser's eruption does a good job of using up all of its water and heat. When that has happened, the geyser must recover by refilling and reheating. Water flowing from the geothermal system below enters the plumbing at a very high temperature. Part of the water boils, which is why geysers always steam, but most just calmly refills the system.

Some geysers will erupt before they are completely full, but in most geysers the surface crater must fill to the very rim with water. Intermittent overflow, some bubbling, and even small splashes will then occur as the entire system continues to heat up. This activity is called *preplay* and may be a good indication of how close the geyser is to its next eruption.

Finally, the geyser is ready. Somewhere within the plumbing system water begins to boil when the continuing inflow from below raises its temperature high enough to overcome the weight of the water column above. A rapid expansion of the steam forces out the remaining water, forming the spouting geyser. Some eruptions begin very suddenly while others are slow to reach their full strength, but once an eruption has been triggered it will continue until one of two things happens.

One possibility is that the geyser will run out of water while there is still enough heat energy to cause boiling. In that case the eruption will merge into a *steam phase*. Liquid water gives way as billowing steam thoroughly empties the geyser's plumbing system.

On the other hand, if the geyser runs short on energy while it still contains plenty of water, the eruption simply stops, often without any warning. This is the case with most geysers because the act of boiling water is a process that consumes energy. Whatever water is left in the crater drains back down to help refill the plumbing system.

Echinus Geyser, at Yellowstone's Norris Geyser Basin, often clearly demonstrates a geyser's cycle of activity. When an eruption ends, water partly drains to a low level within the crater (upper left), *resulting in a calm and cooled pool* (upper right). *In time, as the plumbing system refills and reheats, the pool's level slowly rises* (lower left). *Finally it will overflow* (lower right); *at this point, the geyser is usually near the time of its next eruption*

The *duration* of an eruption, that is, how long it lasts, depends on many things, but primarily it depends on how big a geyser's plumbing system is. Most geysers, large and small, play for only a few minutes, but some have durations of several hours or (very rarely, to be sure) even a few days.

After one eruption has ended, a geyser repeats the entire recovery process during a quiet *interval*. Each geyser has its own unique plumbing system. Some refill in a matter of minutes while others might take months.

Echinus Geyser in eruption.

Does Weather Affect Geysers?

By and large, seasonal climate changes have no effect on geyser activity. Remember that the eruptions are powered by water boiling within plumbing systems at depths of tens to hundreds of feet below the surface. There, the water is completely isolated from the outside world. All other things being equal, geysers are just as active on the coldest winter day as they are under the summer sun.

...iverside Geyser in ...ellowstone's Upper Geyser ...asin in winter (right, NPS ...hoto by George Marler) ...nd in summer. Its activity is ... regular that its eruptions ...an be accurately predicted ... within a few minutes.

The vent of Yellowstone's River Spouter is usually drowned by the Firehole River, but it can spout several feet high when exposed during exceptionally dry years.
—NPS photo by William S. Keller

Although the yearly variations in climate have no effect on geyser activity, daily weather can cause big changes in a few—very few—geysers.

Wind has the most pronounced effect. Some geysers with large surface pools almost never erupt when a strong wind is blowing, and others at least suffer intervals much longer than average. This does not depend on the temperature of the air—the effect is just as strong in summer as in winter. Why this happens is unclear, but in the small number of geysers where this is known to occur, the delay is certain. In Yellowstone, Morning Geyser was so named because it usually plays during the calm morning hours. The same is true of Giantess Geyser, where even a gentle breeze seems to eliminate any potential eruption, and a strong wind will increase Daisy Geyser's intervals by a full 50 percent.

Barometric (or atmospheric) pressure is known to affect some geysers, too. Although not active at all during most years, eruption cycles by Yellowstone's Splendid Geyser are most often triggered when low pressure storm systems pass over the park. And the name of Iceland's Opherrishola translates as "rainmaker" because it almost never plays except during storms.

Cool surface runoff from rain or snowmelt (or possibly a nearby geyser) that flows directly into a geyser crater can thoroughly quench that geyser until the runoff stops. If the flow is persistent over a long period of time, then the drowned spring may be completely sealed, never to erupt again.

Different Kinds of Geysers

Every geyser goes through the same basic eruption process, but because of differences in the near-surface structure of their plumbing systems, eruptions come in three forms: cone-type, fountain-type, and bubble-shower.

Cone-Type Geysers

Most of the better-known geysers are of the cone-type. These often have a geyserite cone at the ground surface, but an actual cone is not required. Just below ground is a very narrow constriction. Cone-type geysers often spray a bit of water during the quiet interval between eruptions, and this constant wetting is what created and caused their cones to grow large through the years.

The small opening acts like a nozzle during an eruption. Cone-type geysers are forceful, jetting steady columns of water to great heights. That's why the cone-type is famous; its examples make up most of the largest geysers worldwide, such as Old Faithful in Yellowstone, Geyser 42w at

Atomizer Geyser in Yellowstone's Upper Geyser Basin is a typical cone-type geyser, erupting with a steady jet of water.

Narcissus Geyser in Yellowstone's Lower Geyser Basin clearly shows the bursting, spraying action of a fountain-type geyser.

Steamboat Hot Springs in Nevada, Wairoa in New Zealand, and Velikan in Kamchatka.

Fountain-Type Geysers

Fountain-type geysers have open craters at the surface that fill with water before or during an eruption. Since the erupting steam must rise through the pool, the action often seems to be weaker than in a cone-type geyser. The steam bubbles cause separate splashes that create a bursting and spraying eruption.

Fountain-type geysers are much more common than the cone-type. Nearly all of the smaller geysers along the trails of Yellowstone are examples, and they are the rule almost without exception in most of the world's other geyser fields. However, fountain-type geysers can be very large. Among the better known are Iceland's Geysir, Yellowstone's Grand and Great Fountain Geysers, New Zealand's Pohutu Geyser, and Kamchatka's Bolshoi Geyser.

The eruptions of bubble-shower springs like Beach Spring in Yellowstone's Upper Geyser Basin consist of boiling at the pool's surface without any evidence of a rising vapor phase. Nevertheless, they clearly undergo intermittent activity, periods of quiet (top) alternating with the boiling eruptions (bottom).

Bubble-Shower Springs

Bubble-shower springs have a controversial status. That they undergo intermittent episodes of vigorous surface boiling because of rapidly rising superheated water (that is, water hotter than the local boiling temperature) is without question, and they therefore look like geysers. However, no vapor phase can be seen rising to the pool's surface, so bubble-shower springs seem to fail that part of the formal definition of a geyser. This leads some scientists to classify them as a variety of intermittent spring rather than as geysers. Undoubtedly, though, there is a vapor phase in the deeper reaches of the plumbing system, and most recent observers include these springs as geysers.

Most bubble-shower springs are relatively small in size, the eruptions sometimes reaching only a few inches high. But there are some large examples. Perhaps the most notable is Yellowstone's Crested Pool, which has boiling eruptions that can reach over 6 feet high.

How Old Are Geysers?

Geothermal systems, being part of long-lived geologic processes, can persist for hundreds of thousands of years. Recent uranium-thorium dating of old sinter deposits near Yellowstone's Canyon Village gave an age of 250,000 years. However, that is an age for the system as a whole, not for the individual hot springs, which are always changing. Figuring out how old a single geyser might be is a difficult task.

The 12-foot-tall geyserite cone of Yellowstone's Castle Geyser is the largest in the world. The cone grew on top of an older geyserite platform that in turn is on top of a wide geyserite mound. The age of the entire structure can only be guessed at but surely amounts to many thousands of years.

It is possible to approximate how long it has taken a cone to form based on its size since geyserite formations often grow less than 1 inch per one hundred years. Large cones, like that of Castle Geyser, are certainly quite old, but a specific figure such as 10,000 years is only a guess.

In some cases there is a better method. Hot springs come and go in time, and an existing spring might have a lengthy inactive period. As soil forms from the geyserite, vegetation develops and trees might grow to be quite large before renewed hot water runoff kills them. New deposits of geyserite then will enclose the old logs and petrify them. This preserved wood can be dated using radioactive carbon-14 in exactly the same way an archaeologist dates an ancient campfire circle.

Old Faithful Geyser's cone had already been damaged by specimen collectors before William Henry Jackson photographed it during the second formal survey of Yellowstone in 1872 (top). The scars on the broken geyserite were still clearly visible when photographed by the author in 1980 (bottom).

Whenever this kind of dating has been done, the results have *not* indicated a great age. The modern Old Faithful Geyser, for example, has been active as a hot spring for only about 750 years. This age does not tell Old Faithful's whole story, though; it is only descriptive of the geyser we see today. Old Faithful's modern deposits are sitting on top of much older geyserite, formed by an earlier spring about which almost nothing is known. Much the same can be said about most other geysers.

The cone formation of Yellowstone's Grotto Geyser scarcely changed in the one hundred years between being photographed by William Henry Jackson in 1871 (top) and the author in 1970 (bottom).

Causes of Changing Geyser Activity

Exchange of Function

You might think that the amount of water and heat flowing into a geyser would always be the same. It rarely is; the water supply to any geyser varies with time. Sometimes the variation is so slight that the geyser is regular and always has nearly the same interval and duration, so its eruptions can be predicted. But more often the variation is greater and the geyser cannot be predicted. No geyser ever really skips an eruption, but it might not erupt for a while when its water and heat are used elsewhere.

Almost all geysers are associated with others in closely related groups. Their plumbing systems are connected below ground and the water source has to supply all of them. Therefore, an eruption by one member of a group affects all the others in mostly unpredictable ways.

On a larger scale, one geyser group can be connected with another similar complex of springs. If one group is active, then the other may be less active or entirely dormant. Relationships of this sort can extend between groups hundreds of feet apart.

This shifting in the water flow is called *exchange of function*. It usually happens suddenly and without warning. Exactly what causes the shift is not known. One idea is that one plumbing system acts as a siphon, drawing water from another. Another cause could be a buildup of steam bubbles somewhere among the connections, acting like a valve. Whatever the reason, exchange of function can cause great variations in the activity of a geyser field, and it is one big reason why one never quite knows what to expect from geysers.

Earthquakes

Earthquakes are frequent in any young volcanic region. Both moderate tremors nearby and major shocks far away are known to cause changes in geyser activity.

On most occasions, Yellowstone's Daisy Geyser (right) in Upper Geyser Basin is active while nearby Splendid Geyser (left) rests as a quiet intermittent spring. Now and then, however, exchange of function shifts the energy within the group of springs so that Splendid erupts one of the park's largest geysers. Rarely, the two geysers will erupt in concert, as they did here in 1987.

In prehistoric time, earthquake tremors created a long fracture through the geyserite near Morning Glory Pool in Yellowstone's Upper Geyser Basin. That crack now hosts Fan Geyser (background right) and Spiteful Geyser (foreground), which formed along the rift by a steam explosion in 1883.

Seismic Geyser in Yellowstone's Upper Geyser Basin owes its entire history to the progressive development of a crack in the ground caused by the Hebgen Lake earthquake in 1959. Its largest eruptions reached over 50 feet high during the 1970s.
—NPS photo by John Brandow in 1970

The Hebgen Lake earthquake of August 17, 1959, centered in Montana just west of Yellowstone National Park, is the prime example. It had a Richter magnitude of about 7.5. Many geysers erupted at the time of the earthquake, often with heights and durations never seen before or since. In the following days hundreds of other hot springs, most of which previously were not known as geysers, also erupted. This increased activity lasted several weeks, and some of the new geysers still haven't died down.

Why these alterations occurred is not clearly understood. The shocks of an earthquake definitely make physical adjustments to the plumbing systems of hot springs. Old springs might erupt if more water is able to flow into them. New geysers are created where open cracks form in the ground.

Other changes are more mysterious. Most of the quiet springs that had eruptions after the Hebgen Lake earthquake have long since quit. They look the same now as they did before. Perhaps the ground motion simply threw or squeezed enough

Earthquake Geyser in Yellowstone's Lower Geyser Basin briefly existed for a few weeks following the 1959 earthquake; some of its eruptions reached 125 feet high. —NPS photo by George Marler

water out of the plumbing system to trigger the odd eruptions. A recent theory speculates that in a process similar to shaking a bottle of soda, the tremors cause the formation of tiny gas bubbles within the plumbing systems, and these alter the flow of water and energy among the geysers. In any case, the springs soon return to normal.

Two things are certain: all geyser fields have experienced and will continue to experience a lot of earthquakes, and every time a big earthquake shakes the ground, there will be new geysers to see.

Disturbances

The passing seasons can affect geysers, not because of weather conditions—geysers are just as active when the temperature is fifty below zero as in midsummer—but because of variations in the local water supply.

It might seem that long periods of drought could decrease the number of geysers in an area or their eruptions. After all, their water does begin as precipitation; if it isn't present to enter the system, then it can't come out. However, no strong

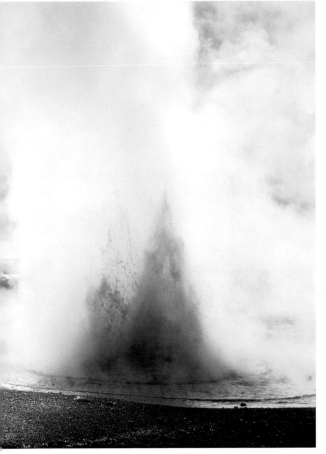

Eruptions by Pinto Geyser are rare except when the Norris Geyser Basin is experiencing a disturbance. Then it may erupt as high as 45 feet.

Usually a calm, muddy spring deep within a crater, Congress Pool sometimes turns into a significant geyser during a disturbance in Yellowstone's Norris Geyser Basin.

evidence links even long-term drought to a decrease in geyser eruptions. It is likely that yearly variations in water supply are averaged out during the long percolation through a geothermal system. The total amount of hot water available seems to be almost constant.

But seasonal changes, called *disturbances*, may affect almost every spring and geyser within an entire geyser basin. Cool near-surface groundwater can mix with hotter, deeper geothermal water in any geyser basin. In late summer there is less cool water and so less mixing. The water available to the springs might be a smaller volume, but it is hotter. Increased boiling opens clogged channels that have been sealed in, and new springs appear. The water is muddy. Quiet pools erupt violently, while existing geysers have larger and more-frequent eruptions. The entire area is animated until the system adjusts itself to the new flow. Things usually return to normal after a few days, but some disturbance changes can be permanent.

Plume Geyser near Old Faithful acted as a cone-type geyser (left, in 1970) until a small steam explosion enlarged its crater in 1972. Now (right, in 1990) it behaves as a fountain-type geyser.

Steam Explosions

Water is an excellent explosive. Just 1 gallon of liquid water boiled completely will yield more than 1,500 gallons of vapor. This explosive potential exists only when the water is kept superheated and under confining pressure—the exact situation found within the underground cavities inside geyser plumbing systems.

An ordinary eruption accomodates the pressure increase caused by boiling water in a geyser. But sometimes the pressure is too much for the rock lining the plumbing to withstand. When it breaks, the geyserite explodes apart, leaving behind a crater.

It is believed that most, possibly all, Yellowstone hot springs formed in this way, but only a few steam blasts have occurred in recorded times. In 1884, an early Yellowstone tour guide wrote that "The Spiteful stones unwary heads," apparently describing the 1883 explosion that created the jagged crater of Spiteful Geyser that we see today. In 1972, beautiful Plume Geyser near Old Faithful blew out a second and a third vent, dramatically changing the appearance of its eruptions. Still more impressive was the 1989 disruption of Porkchop Geyser at Yellowstone's Norris Geyser Basin, whose explosion threw huge blocks of broken geyserite more than 200 feet, and the 1934 blast

...orkchop Geyser in Yellowstone's Norris Geyser Basin was a small ...ring that occasionally erupted a thin jet of water a few feet high ...t often was just a quiet pool (left, in 1972). After a period of ...creasingly strong and steady eruptions, in 1989 Porkchop exploded ...d threw chunks of geyserite more than 200 feet. Now a pool that ...ccasionally boils occupies the jagged crater (right, in 1990).

Black Opal Pool in Yellowstone's Upper Geyser Basin was formed by a titanic steam explosion in 1934. No known person witnessed the event that threw boulders of rock as far as 500 feet.

that created Upper Geyser Basin's Black Opal Pool by throwing chunks of sandstone that weighed hundreds of pounds apiece as far as 500 feet.

Unknown Events

All changes in geyser activity must have some specific cause, but often the triggering event is not known. Commonly, a spring not previously known as a geyser erupts once or a few times and has no observable effect on nearby springs. These surprise eruptions might result from a gradual accumulation of excess heat within the plumbing system, which finally reaches a critical point. A brief series of eruptions is enough to return the spring to its normal quiet state. Other changes in activity might be a result of a slight exchange of function, or some other variation in the water supply that would otherwise be invisible. The precipitation of new geyserite or the enlargement of a tiny fracture within a plumbing system might also cause substantial alterations in the flow of water.

Butterfly Spring in Yellowstone's Upper Geyser Basin, known only for rare minor eruptions during the 1880s and again in 1936, became a major geyser during the single month of May 2003. Some of its muddy water jets reached over 50 feet high. The cause of the activity is completely unknown, as no nearby spring appeared to be affected in any way.

Fantail Geyser was mysteriously active only between April and October 1986, but during that short time it underwent frequent eruptions that were up to 75 feet high.

These spontaneous changes in geyser activity are usually temporary, and they are certainly never predictable. The results, however, can be very spectacular, giving brief existence to large geysers. Perhaps there is no better example of this than the activity of Fantail Geyser in Yellowstone's Upper Geyser Basin. Fantail was a superheated pool until April 1986 when its eruptions reached 75 feet high, took place as often as every six hours, and lasted more than forty-five minutes each. Less than six months later, Fantail had reverted to a gently boiling pool, and so it remains. Only one small nearby hot spring was affected at the same time, so the cause of this activity is completely unknown.

Regular Cyclic Processes

On occasion, researchers have found evidence that geyser activity is controlled, at least to a slight degree, by either one of two physical processes that go through predictably regular variations.

First is the simple difference between day and night, known as *diurnal variations*. As the temperature cools at night, the temperature of surface water runoff may in turn cool. If the cooled water flows into a plumbing system network, it may slow or completely quench geyser activity. Although apparently observed in a few geysers, the effect has never been reliable or predictable.

Second is the measurable and predictable monthly cycle of *tidal variations* caused by the gravitational forces of the Moon and Sun. At the times of the new moon and full moon phases, when the Earth, Moon, and Sun are in alignment, tidal stresses are at their greatest. Theoretically, this should tug on geyser plumbing systems, increasing water circulation and decreasing subsurface pressure, thereby allowing boiling that otherwise might not take place. Eruptions should be more frequent. Again, this is an effect that has been observed at times, but mostly in drilled geothermal wells rather than natural springs. Gravitational influences on geyser activity are, at best, highly controversial.

External Environmental Events

It is entirely possible for seemingly ordinary events to affect geysers. One of Yellowstone's most dramatic examples of this occurred at Gibbon Hill Geyser in

Gibbon Hill Geyser, a vigorous little geyser surrounded by a massive, intricately decorated geyserite formation (top), was destroyed (bottom) when a thunderstorm in 1989 triggered a landslide from the denuded slopes of Gibbon Hill, which had burned in the 1988 forest fires.

48

a backcountry area. Once one of the more-beautiful springs in the park, its crater was filled with muddy debris during a landslide that was triggered by a thunderstorm following the forest fires of 1988. The geyser has never recovered. However, a nearby spring that previously had been observed as an empty crater is now active as a geyser—an exchange of function forced by a landslide. It has been named Phoenix Geyser.

Human Activities

Natural events help geysers remain fresh and dynamic. Geology acts slowly, and while individual geysers are always evolving, there will still be geysers tens of thousands of years into the future—if people allow them to exist. Intentionally or by accident, people damage delicate geyser systems. They are easy to destroy.

Throwing objects into a geyser (or any other kind of hot spring) may ruin it. Rocks and coins settle into the bottom opening of a crater; sticks get waterlogged and also drop into the vent. Any foreign debris will be fastened into place by new geyserite and cannot be removed. The spring may be completely sealed in. Its water will still reach the surface, but somewhere else. When this happens, a geyser is lost, a pool will become cooler and less beautiful, or a fumarole will die. Making a wish in a hot spring or geyser is a poor and destructive idea.

The thirty or more geysers that existed at Beowawe, Nevada, were once proposed for national park status. Now Beowawe has no geysers at all; the Whirlwind Valley geothermal power plant, constructed in 1986, destroyed every one.

Even distant activity can have an effect. In Iceland, New Zealand, Nevada, and elsewhere geothermal drilling for power plants has destroyed many geysers. The inflow of water to a natural geothermal area might be many miles from the geysers. When a well is drilled that intercepts the supply of a geyser field, the water that produces the geysers may be diverted. If the Yellowstone system were to be developed in the same way, the results would be disastrous to the geysers there.

Ebony Geyser was once one of the more-vigorous geysers at Yellowstone's Norris Geyser Basin, but it has not erupted since the early 1970s because its vent is choked by rocks thrown by people. —NPS photo, photographer unknown

Safety Among Geysers

Sometimes it is difficult to imagine just how hot the water of these springs really is. So remember: geysers erupt because of boiling water, and the boiling water in the geyser basins is just as hot as that on your stove at home. Far more than hot enough for cooking, it will give you a severe burn in only a fraction of a second. It isn't a pleasant thought, but it is well worth knowing that more Yellowstone tourists have been killed by the hot springs than by all bear, bison, moose, and other animal incidents combined.

In Yellowstone, New Zealand, Kamchatka, and parts of Iceland, at Hot Creek in California's Long Valley Caldera, and in most of the other more-important geyser fields, boardwalks and trails have been constructed into the thermal areas. They are not there for show, but for your safety and for the protection of the hot springs themselves. STAY ON THE WALK!

In less well-developed areas and in the more remote parts of places like Yellowstone, such walkways have not been built. The hazards there are no less real. Whenever there is not a walk, a simple and handy rule serves as a good guide—keep yourself a body length away from the nearest hot spring, and always show concern for the fragile deposits of geyserite.

Boardwalks help protect both you and the geysers. Please stay on them at all times, as this crowd is doing at Beehive Geyser.

Geyser Fields of the World

Fields listed according to continent and country. The number of active geysers is per the best available information in 2004.

NORTH AMERICA

Geyser fields in North America are of diverse geological origins. Subduction of oceanic plates beneath the North American Plate is responsible for those of mainland Mexico (Cocos Plate), northern California (Juan de Fuca Plate), and the Aleutian Islands of Alaska (Pacific Plate). Geysers in Baja California, Mexico, and southern California are associated with the pull-apart zone that separates the North American and Pacific Plates. Geysers in Nevada and Oregon are where the North American Plate is stretched and thinned. Yellowstone, Wyoming, and Long Valley, California, are above hot spots, where plumes of magma rise from deep within the Earth.

LOCATION	NUMBER OF KNOWN GEYSERS	DESCRIPTION
United States		
Yellowstone National Park, Wyoming	500	World's largest geyser field with as many as five hundred geysers active in any year and more than eight hundred in recorded times.
Geyser Bight, Umnak Island, Aleutian Chain, Alaska	9	Remote and accessible only by boat, these small springs have only recently been visited by Alaska state geologists; the geysers are all quite small, but their activity is vigorous.
Morgan Springs, adjacent to Lassen Volcanic National Park, California	5 (?)	Located within closely guarded private property where research access is routinely denied; one definite geyser was active in 1925, and five geysers and/or perpetual spouters were active in 1955.
Kanaga Island, Aleutian Chain, Alaska	4 (?)	Within an area formerly involved in nuclear weapons testing, the boiling and erupting hot springs have been given scant attention by the U.S. Geological Survey.
Hot Creek, Long Valley Caldera, Mammoth Lakes, California	3	Geysers up to 30 feet high have been observed shortly after large earthquakes, but their activity quickly decreases to weak, intermittent boiling; nearby Little Hot Creek and Casa Diablo have also been known as the sites of small but scarcely observed geysers.
Great Boiling Springs, Gerlach, Nevada	3	First described by Captain John C. Fremont in 1845, this was the site of three small bubble-shower geysers in 1986, but none were observed in 2004.
Mickey Hot Springs, Oregon	1	One small geyser discovered in 1986.
Beowawe, Nevada	extinct	Once the site of at least thirty geysers and proposed as a national park, the geysers were altered by geothermal drilling in the 1950s and 1960s, and then destroyed by the construction of the Whirlwind Valley geothermal power plant, which began operating in 1986.

The five largest geyser fields (stars) and all other known fields (dots) of the world.

LOCATION	NUMBER OF KNOWN GEYSERS	DESCRIPTION
Steamboat Hot Springs, Nevada	extinct	Just south of Reno, much of the research about how geysers and geothermal systems operate was conducted here before the twenty or more geysers were destroyed by the construction of a power plant during 1986–1987.
Lassen Volcanic National Park, California	extinct (?)	Terminal Geyser, in a small thermal area at the southeast corner of the national park, was definitely active during the 1870s and 1920s, but usually as a perpetual spouter; nearby but outside the park boundary a geothermal test well was drilled in the 1980s, and it may have affected the spring's activity.
Hell's Kitchen, Salton Sea, California	extinct (?)	Numerous small geysers as well as erupting mud pots existed near the volcanic dome of Mullett Island, at the southeast corner of Salton Sea; the area is now under shallow water and, if exposed, could reactivate.

Mexico

LOCATION	NUMBER OF KNOWN GEYSERS	DESCRIPTION
Comanjilla, Estado Guanajuato	11	These small geysers are all within the fenced grounds of a hot spring resort hotel, whose management fortunately appreciates the rarity of the geysers and encourages visitation.
Ixtlan de los Hervores, Estado Michoacan	2	Promoted as "Mexico's Little Yellowstone," this was the location of at least fourteen geysers before most were destroyed by geothermal drilling for a power plant that was never built.
Cerro Prieto, Estado Baja California Norte	1 (?)	Geysers erupting up to 200 feet high were observed after several large earthquakes in the 1800s and early 1900s (most recently in 1934); since then, at least one geyser erupting 30 feet high was observed throughout the 1990s despite a nearby geothermal power plant.

SOUTH AMERICA

All the geyser fields of South America are within the volcanic Andes Mountains and are caused by the subduction of the Nazca Plate beneath the South American Plate.

Chile

LOCATION	NUMBER OF KNOWN GEYSERS	DESCRIPTION
El Tatio, El Loa Province, Antofagasta Region	85	The world's third-largest geyser field is in the Andes Mountains at an elevation of 13,800 feet above sea level; the largest geyser only erupts about 20 feet high; geothermal drilling has occurred, and the geysers are threatened by future power plant developments.
Puchuldiza and Tuja, Iquique Province, Tarapacá Region	8	In a setting similar to El Tatio but threatened by both large-scale gold mining and geothermal drilling, four geysers have been reported in each of these areas that lie 4 miles apart.
Polloquere, Salar de Suriri, Parinacota Province, Tarapacá Region	1	One boiling geyser within a national reserve.

Peru

LOCATION	NUMBER OF KNOWN GEYSERS	DESCRIPTION
Carumas, General Sanchez Cerro Province, Moquegua Region	8	Although some geysers were lost when recently flooded by an irrigation reservoir, at least eight geysers remain among hot spring groups scattered along the Rio Putina.

LOCATION	NUMBER OF KNOWN GEYSERS	DESCRIPTION
Peru *cont.*		
Calientes Candarave, Candarave Province, Tacna Region	1	Hot springs scattered over a wide area.
Puentebello, Lampas Province, Puno Region	1	Perpetual spouters and one geyser within a cavern.
Argentina		
Domuyo Protected Natural Area, Neuquén Territory	8	Geysers definitely exist at Villa Aguas Calientes and Los Olletas, and possibly also among other thermal groups a few miles away.
Bolivia		
several possible places in Andes Mountains	several (?)	Geysers have been described among several hot spring areas high in the Andes Mountains, but no details have been recorded; the setting is geologically identical to that in the mountains of adjacent Chile, where geysers occur in at least three localities, but at least one Bolivian site (Sol de Mañana) is now known to include only mud pots and perpetual spouters but no true geysers.

ATLANTIC OCEAN

Iceland and the Azores Islands have formed along the Mid-Atlantic Ridge, the pull-apart zone that separates the North American and Eurasian Plates.

LOCATION	NUMBER OF KNOWN GEYSERS	DESCRIPTION
Iceland		
several scattered areas	30	World's fifth-largest geyser field; Geysir, the namesake of all geysers, is at Haukadalur, where there has been some preservation of the area's hot springs, but most other hot spring areas have been altered or destroyed.
Portugal		
Volcan Furnas, São Miguel Island, Azores Islands	3 (?)	True geysers, perhaps of large size, probably existed circa 1900, but recent reports imply that they now boil steadily because of alterations made for resort use.

AFRICA (including Turkey)

Geyser fields in Kenya and Ethiopia are within the East Africa rift valley, the pull-apart zone where the African Plate is being split into two smaller, new plates. Geysers in Chad probably lie at a hot spot above a mantle plume.. The geyser in Turkey is listed here because it is isolated from all others and associated with the subduction of the African Plate under the Eurasian Plate.

LOCATION	NUMBER OF KNOWN GEYSERS	DESCRIPTION
Kenya		
Loburu, Chemurkeu, and others, Lake Bogoria	13	A little-known field in central Kenya; small geysers scattered among four hot spring groups along the lakeshore.
Logkippi Geyser, Elboitong Valley	extinct (?)	Almost never visited but active when visited throughout the 1800s and 1900s; Logkippi was recently found to be inactive, probably because of dropping groundwater levels due to an ongoing regional drought.

LOCATION	NUMBER OF KNOWN GEYSERS	DESCRIPTION
Ethiopia		
Allallobeda, Danakil Region	1	One geyser among several boiling pools.
Lakes Abaya and Langano	unknown	Geysers definitely exist in thermal areas around these lakes in southern Ethiopia (including on Geyser Island within Geyser Bay in Lake Langano), but no comprehensive report has provided detailed information about how many or how extensive the geysers might be.
Chad		
Pic Tousside, Yirrigue Caldera, Tibesti Mountains	unknown	Geysers have been reported to exist among hot springs on this dormant volcano, but details have never been recorded; the entire mountain range is closed to entry due to antigovernment rebels and land mines.
Turkey		
Ayvacik	1	Gayzer Suyu possibly described in Homer's Iliad.

EAST ASIA

Geysers in east Asia are of diverse origins. The fields in China, Myanmar, and Thailand are in a zone of compression where the Indian and Australian Plates are colliding with the Eurasian Plate. Geysers in Indonesia are along the subduction zone between the Australian and Eurasian Plates—the same zone that produced the devastating magnitude 9 earthquake and tsunami in late 2004. Geysers in the Philippines and southern Japan are where the Philippine Plate is being subducted under the Eurasian Plate, and those of northern Japan and Russia are where the Pacific Plate is being subducted beneath the North American Plate.

LOCATION	NUMBER OF KNOWN GEYSERS	DESCRIPTION
China		
Tagajia, Xizang (Tibet)	4	Cone-type geysers spout water up to 40 feet high from a geyserite terrace adjacent to the main east-west highway of Xizang.
Chaluo, Sichuan	4	Probably several more small geysers exist in addition to the four listed in a government geothermal resources report.
Chapu, Xizang (Tibet)	2	As with other Chinese localities, there likely are more than two geysers at Chapu.
Kunlun Shan, Xizang (Tibet)	many (?)	A Chinese report published in 2002 about a geological expedition to the mountains on the far northern edge of Xizang reported "many" geysers and related the region to Yellowstone National Park, but no specifics about the geysers were given.
Guhu, Xizang (Tibet)	unknown	As with other Chinese localities, Guhu is barely noted by Chinese literature as the site of geysers.
Rehai, Yunnan	1	One geyser specifically reported; others may exist.
Myanmar (Burma)		
Pai, Tavoy District	1	Possibly more than one geyser in the area. (Described as within Burma during the 1800s, this locality may be within modern Thailand, where there are boiling springs near a town named Pai.)
Lashio, Fang District	1	A single geyser is an advertised attraction within a park near the town.

LOCATION	NUMBER OF KNOWN GEYSERS	DESCRIPTION
Thailand		
Chiang Mai and Mae Hong Son	19	World's sixth-largest geyser field; small geysers exist at a number of poorly documented hot spring areas in the northern provinces of Thailand. The best-known geysers are at San Kamphaeng, a resort area near the city of Chiang Mai.
Indonesia		
Lampung-Semangko District, Sumatra	3	At the eastern tip of Sumatra, the area contains hundreds of boiling springs and possibly more than three geysers.
Tapanuli, Sumatra	2	Reported without detail in a 1972 geothermal resources report.
Volcan Kerinci, Sumatra	1	Reportedly active in dry weather only, when it is 50 feet high.
Pasaman, Sumatra	1	Listed in a 1982 personal letter to T. Scott Bryan as having one geyser.
Bacan Island, Maluku Group	1	One large geyser named Atoe Ri described before 1900.
Bukapeting, Alor Island	several	The geysers found during a geothermal reconnaissance in the late 1980s were only mentioned in passing in a geothermal report published in 1998.
Minahasa District, Sulawesi (Celebes) Island	several	The geysers at Airmadidi have been destroyed by the development of a geothermal power plant, but a few geysers exist in at least three other places near the northeastern tip of Sulawesi.
Cisolok, Java Island	2 (?)	Two springs that spout 15 feet high were described as true geysers by an Indonesian volcanologist but as perpetual spouters by a New Zealand geologist.
Gunung Papandayan, Java Island	unknown	Travel guidebooks have noted geysers in the area of this frequently active volcano, which is a popular hiking area for international trekkers.
Philippines		
Tongonan, Leyte Island	extinct	Erupting as much as 15 feet high, the several geysers at Tongonan ceased activity when a nearby geothermal power plant began operating in 1997.
Japan		
Onikobe, Miyagi Prefecture, Honshū Island	2	Japan's only known remaining geyser field (at least four others have been destroyed); even here geothermal developments have altered most hot springs and only two small geysers remain active.
Beppu, Oita Prefecture, Kyūshū Island	unknown	Several intermittently erupting features exist within the resort city of Beppu, where boiling springs certainly existed before resort development took place. At least some of these "geysers" are now known to be drilled wells, and how many natural geysers exist is unknown.
Russia		
Dolina Geizerov, Kamchatka Peninsula	200	The world's second-largest geyser field is within the Kronotsky Nature Reserve, first visited by Americans in 1991; most of the geysers are smaller butmore-vigorously active than those of Yellowstone.
Pauzhetsk, Kamchatka Peninsula	2 (?)	In the southern part of the Kamchatka Peninsula, two geysers are reported to persist despite the nearby construction of a geothermal power plant.

LOCATION	NUMBER OF KNOWN GEYSERS	DESCRIPTION
Russia *cont.*		
Shiashkotan Island, Kuril Islands	unknown	Although referred to as "The Island of a Thousand Geysers" in Russian literature, the only detailed description of the springs clearly describes just one erupting pool.

ISLANDS IN THE SOUTHWEST PACIFIC

Geyser fields in this region are all located along the subduction zone where the Pacific Plate is colliding with the Australian Plate.

LOCATION	NUMBER OF KNOWN GEYSERS	DESCRIPTION
New Zealand		
Rotorua, Taupo, and vicinity, central North Island	70	World's fourth-largest geyser field; recent environmental awareness led to the preservation of several geyser areas, most notably at Whakarewarewa near Rotorua, but human activities have destroyed at least two hundred geysers.
Fiji		
Nakama Springs, Savusavu, Vanua Levu Island	5	Actually within the town limits, this tiny area (only 60 feet long) boasts several springs that undergo boiling eruptions only inches to 2 feet high; jetting geysers up to 60 feet high were seen during the 1800s.
Solomon Islands		
Vutusuala Hot Springs, Savo Island	several	This thermal area is said to be a "wonderland of small geysers."
Papua New Guinea		
Koimumu (Kasiloli), New Britain Island	14	Until recently, closed to public entry due to the presence of megapode birds that incubate their eggs by geothermal heat instead of nesting; now open to guided tours; geyser count as of 1955.
Deidei and Iamelele, d'Entrecasteaux Islands	12	Two areas near one another on Fergusson Island off the eastern tip of New Guinea; the geysers have appeared in British television documentary programs and are now promoted to tourists.
Kapkai, Ambitle Island (Feni Islands)	7	Hot springs in two areas, one within a copra plantation where there are two small geysers, and the other in the nearby hills where one pool splashes up to 30 feet high, another reaches 6 feet, and at least three others splash from pools.
Pangalu, New Britain Island	2	Two intermittently erupting vents within deep craters; across Garua Harbor, there may be small geysers among the numerous boiling springs within the town of Talasea.
Lihir Island	extinct	There were four geysers within a volcanic crater on Lihir, but the geyserite contains significant copper and silver, and mining destroyed the hot springs.

Glossary

algae. Colonial, single-celled plants; in geothermal areas, true algae are common in cold stream and lake water but are uncommon in geothermal water unless it is thoroughly cooled and/or is acidic. See also *cyanobacteria*.

boiling springs. Any hot spring that boils at Earth's surface, including geysers and perpetual spouters but also many springs that never actually erupt or show intermittent action.

bubble-shower spring. A geyser with an eruption that consists of intermittent episodes of violent boiling as superheated water surges to the surface of a pool.

calorie. The amount of heat energy necessary to raise the temperature of 1 gram of water by 1 degree Celsius (centigrade); by conversion, it takes about 250 calories to raise the temperature of 1 pound of water by 1 degree Fahrenheit.

cone. A built-up formation of geyserite on the ground surface, within which is the geyser's vent.

cone-type geyser. A geyser with an eruption that is jetted as a steady column of mixed water and steam from a small vent either within a cone or at least from an area with little or no surface pool.

crater. May be synonymous with *vent*, but more typically refers to an open pit or depression often containing a pool, at the bottom of which is a hot spring vent.

cyanobacteria. A variety of primitive, thermophilic chlorophyll-bearing bacteria that survive in alkaline geothermal water at temperatures below 167 degrees Fahrenheit. Previously known as "blue-green algae" but distinct from true algae in that a cyanobacterium has no nucleus in its cell.

dead. Extinct; a hot spring or geyser that is not and never again will be active. Use this term with extreme caution because many hot springs that appear dead are really only dormant.

diurnal variations. Changes in geyser or other hot spring activity because of the physical differences between daytime and nighttime.

dormant. The term used to describe a geyser or other hot spring that is not presently active. It is not the same as *dead* or *extinct*, terms that must be used with great caution.

duration. How long a geyser eruption lasts; that is, the time from the beginning of one eruption to the end of the same eruption.

exchange of function. The shift of energy and/or water from one geyser, other hot spring feature, or hot spring group to another, resulting in a decline of activity in the first and an increase in the other.

extinct. Dead, with no possibility of future activity. Often incorrectly used as a synonym for *dormant*.

fountain-type geyser. A geyser with an eruption that is a series of separate bursts of water, usually issuing from a pool with a vent within a crater.

fumarole. A steam vent; that is, a hot spring in which all available water is converted to steam at depth before reaching Earth's surface.

geothermal. The term applied to any geological system or process that relies on Earth's internal heat as the source of its energy.

geyser. A hot spring that erupts intermittently because of the boiling of water within the confining spaces of a plumbing system below Earth's surface.

geyser basin. An area of hot springs within which one or more geysers is found.

geyser field. A geographical region that contains one or more geyser basins. Yellowstone National Park, for example, is one geyser field within which there are nine major and several minor geyser basins.

geyserite. The variety of opaline silica (hydrated silicon dioxide) that is deposited by the water of high-temperature geothermal systems; also known as *siliceous sinter*. It is different from travertine, a common hot spring deposit composed of calcium carbonate.

hot spot. A volcanic area that lies above a plume of magma that rises from deep within Earth

hydrogen sulfide. The volcanic gas emitted from hot springs that causes the rotten-egg odor of thermal areas.

intermittent spring. A hot spring that undergoes occasional episodes of quiet overflow without a bursting or jetting eruption.

interval. The amount of time between geyser eruptions; that is, the time from the end of one eruption to the beginning of the next eruption. In practice, however, used as a synonym for *period*.

magma. Molten rock that exists at any depth below Earth's surface.

mud pot. An acidic hot spring with a limited water supply; not enough water is present to carry away clay mud that forms from chemical and bacterial alteration of the rocks of the crater.

mud volcano. A mud pot whose mud is so thick that it piles up in a volcanolike shape around the vent.

paint pot. A mud pot in which the mud is so fluid that it has a paintlike consistency.

period. The interval plus the duration; that is, the time from the start of one eruption to the start of the next eruption. Compare with *interval*.

perpetual spouter. An erupting spring that resembles a geyser except that its eruption does not stop.

plumbing system. The subsurface network of tubes, cavities, and channels that makes up the immediate water supply system of any hot spring; it is especially important for geysers in that it must include a near-surface constriction, be pressure tight, and be accessible to large volumes of superheated water.

pool. The term applied to a noneruptive hot spring that has an open body of water within a crater; also, the body of water that occupies the crater of a fountain-type geyser during the interval between eruptions.

pull-apart zone. A boundary between tectonic plates where divergence causes the plates to move away from each other.

sinter. The general term for any mineral deposit formed by hot water. In Yellowstone and most other geyser fields, it is the siliceous sinter or geyserite composed of hydrated silicon dioxide (a form of opal) that is of greatest importance. In other areas there are sinters of travertine, composed of calcium carbonate, and sinters of iron oxide.

subduction zone. A boundary between tectonic plates of Earth's crust where convergence causes one plate to bend and slide beneath the other.

superheated. Referring to the water of a geyser, hotter than the surface boiling temperature (about 198 degrees Fahrenheit in Yellowstone National Park).

tectonic plate. Any one of the solid slabs of Earth's crust that move relative to one another, sometimes converging at subduction zones and elsewhere diverging at pull-apart zones.

thermophilic. Literally "heat loving," the term used in reference to the communities of primitive bacteria, algae, and animals that live in or on hot spring water.

vapor phase. The release—by a hot spring—of gases such as steam, hydrogen sulfide, and carbon dioxide without the presence of liquid water.

vent. The surface opening of the plumbing system of any hot spring; in geysers it is the point from which an eruption issues, usually located within a cone or at the bottom of a crater.

In recent times, Steamboat Geyser at the Norris Geyser Basin has erupted just one to three times per year, but when it plays it is the largest geyser in the world. Its water jets have been measured as tall as 386 feet. —NPS photo by R. Lang and W. Dick

Steamboat Geyser almost looks like the smoke plume of a forest fire when viewed from Elk Park nearly a mile away.
—NPS photo by Luis Gastellum

Other Sources of Information

Allen, E. T., and A. L. Day. 1935. *Hot Springs of the Yellowstone National Park.* Carnegie Institution of Washington, Publication Number 466.

Brock, T. D. 1994. *Life at High Temperatures.* Yellowstone National Park: Yellowstone Association.

Bryan, T. S. 2001. *The Geysers of Yellowstone*, 3rd ed. Boulder, Colorado: University Press of Colorado.

Christiansen, R. L. 2001. *The Quaternary and Pliocene Yellowstone Plateau volcanic field of Wyoming, Idaho, and Montana.* U.S. Geological Survey, Professional Paper 729-G.

Fournier, R. O. 1989. Geochemistry and dynamics of the Yellowstone National Park hydrothermal system. *Annual Review of Earth and Planetary Sciences* 17:13–53.

Keefer, W. R. 1971. *The Geologic Story of Yellowstone National Park.* U.S. Geological Survey, Bulletin 1347.

Marler, G. D. 1969. *The Story of Old Faithful Geyser.* Yellowstone National Park: The Yellowstone Association.

Marler, G. D. 1973. *Inventory of Thermal Features of the Firehole River Geyser Basins and Other Selected Areas of Yellowstone National Park.* U.S. Department of Commerce, National Technical Information Service, Publication Number PB-221289 for U.S. Geological Survey; reproduced by the Geyser Observation and Study Association.

Smith, R. B., and L. J. Siegel. 2000. *Windows into the Earth: The Geologic Story of Yellowstone and Grand Teton National Parks.* London: Oxford University Press.

White, D. E., R. A. Hutchinson, and T. E. C. Keith. 1988. *The geology and remarkable thermal activity of Norris Geyser Basin, Yellowstone National Park, Wyoming.* U.S. Geological Survey, Professional Paper 1456.

Whittlesey, L. H. 1989. *Wonderland Nomenclature: A History of the Place Names of Yellowstone National Park.* Helena: Montana Historical Society Press, cooperatively reproduced by the Geyser Observation and Study Association.

Members of the Geyser Observation and Study Association (at upper left) *watch Avalanche Geyser in Yellowstone's backcountry.*

The Geyser Observation and Study Association

The Geyser Observation and Study Association (GOSA) was established in 1988 as a nonprofit scientific and educational corporation. Its major goals are to increase and improve the accumulation of data so as to enhance the general understanding of geysers, and to disseminate this information to the general public. Commonly known as *geyser gazers* and numbering more than four hundred strong, GOSA members mostly watch the geysers for their own enjoyment, but they also report their observations in formal publications and aid the National Park Service by providing tremendous amounts of data to the park's research staff and archives.

GOSA publishes a bimonthly newsletter containing updates on the geysers, organization news, and topical articles. Occasional volumes called the *GOSA Transactions* include longer research articles. While most geyser gazers concentrate on Yellowstone, GOSA's scope and membership is international.

Geyser gazing is fun and gazers enjoy parties, but GOSA is not a social club. Serious new geyser gazers are encouraged to join and contribute to our knowledge. The organization's officers and mailing addresses sometimes change, but general information is always available at the organization's Internet Web site, www.geyserstudy.org, and often from the active gazers you might encounter in Yellowstone.

Index

About the Author

T. Scott Bryan earned degrees in geological sciences at San Diego State University (BS 1972) and the University of Montana (MS 1974). He spent fourteen summers working in Yellowstone National Park and later served in the Volunteer in Parks program. He is the author of *The Geysers of Yellowstone* (University Press of Colorado). Scott was one of the founding directors—and the first president—of the Geyser Observation and Study Association. He presently edits the *GOSA Transactions*, a series of volumes that compile geyser-related research papers.

Bryan retired as professor of geology and astronomy at Victor Valley College in Victorville, California, in 2001. During the winter he serves as a docent and education mentor at the Living Desert in Palm Desert, California. In summer he frequents Yellowstone's geysers from a residence in West Yellowstone, Montana. With his wife, Betty Tucker-Bryan, he is coauthor of *The Explorer's Guide to Death Valley National Park*, his other favorite national park.

T. Scott Bryan and his wife, Betty

In addition to *Geysers: What They Are and How They Work, 2nd Edition*, Mountain Press Publishing Company publishes a series of Roadside Geology guides, Roadside History guides, full-color plant and bird guides, outdoor guides, horse books, and a wide selection of western Americana titles, as well as The Tumbleweed Series—reprints of classic cowboy short stories and novels by the famed artist and storyteller Will James.

For more information about our books, please give us a call at 800-234-5308 or mail us your address and we will happily send you a catalog. If you have a friend who would like to receive our catalog, simply include his or her name and address. Thank you for your interest in our titles and for supporting an independent press devoted to providing high-quality books to readers interested in the world around them.

Name_____

Address_____

City / State / Zip_____

Mountain Press Publishing Company
P.O. Box 2399 • Missoula, MT 59806
phone: 406-728-1900 • fax: 406-728-1635
toll free: 1-800-234-5308
e-mail: info@mtnpress.com
web: www.mountain-press.com